WHEN
GOD
ARRESTED
ME

WHEN GOD ARRESTED ME

When Freedom Become Free

CHARITY JOHNSON

iUniverse®

WHEN GOD ARRESTED ME
WHEN FREEDOM BECOME FREE

iUniverse books may be ordered through booksellers or by contacting:

iUniverse
1663 Liberty Drive
Bloomington, IN 47403
www.iuniverse.com
844-349-9409

Because of the dynamic nature of the Internet, any web addresses or links contained in this book may have changed since publication and may no longer be valid. The views expressed in this work are solely those of the author and do not necessarily reflect the views of the publisher, and the publisher hereby disclaims any responsibility for them.

Any people depicted in stock imagery provided by Getty Images are models, and such images are being used for illustrative purposes only. Certain stock imagery © Getty Images.

ISBN: 978-1-6632-6658-3 (sc)
ISBN: 978-1-6632-6660-6 (hc)
ISBN: 978-1-6632-6659-0 (e)

Library of Congress Control Number: 2024918307

Print information available on the last page.

iUniverse rev. date: 10/14/2024

1

ONE SUMMER EVENING IN THE MONTH OF AUGUST, I was walking up my hallway, about to enter the living room, when suddenly something came over me. It was an uncontrollable urge to just start doing something, but I didn't know what to do. I started to talk out openly and honestly to God. The best way to describe it might be that it was as if someone had suddenly come into my house, taken my hands, and lifted them up in the air for me.

At the time, I was so addicted to cocaine and alcohol that I didn't realize just how sad and pitiful my life had become. I was so messed up and out of touch with reality that I could determine neither the level of my sickness and my pain nor that I was in a deep state of depression. I even attempted suicide and failed. All I knew was that I was full of anger, mad as hell with myself because of the world I had created for myself. My world and my reality, yet not the truth.

But on that day, something started happening to me from the inside. I started behaving like someone who had suddenly come under the control of a powerful yet wonderful force, a force that started to control my body, my mind, and my words. It was as if words were coming out of my mouth that I didn't even have to think about to say them. I was so affected that I started to feel as if I was an alien from another planet or something. It was like nothing I'd experienced before.

It was the manifest presence of God, and it was so strong right there in my living room that it felt like I was going to take wings and fly off somewhere. I was not afraid; in fact, I was amazed and overwhelmed with joy at the very thought that God Himself would show up in my living room. I had never imagined it was possible to experience Him in that way. I had never heard anyone say that God makes personal visits. I didn't know He did anything like that, but it became obvious to me right then that I seriously needed and wanted Him there in my tired, lifeless life. I say "lifeless life" because while I was hearing, seeing, touching, smelling, and tasting with all five senses in operation, I was dead to the reality of life. I was no longer living but only existing from day to day.

You see, even though I was still on this earth, I was so lost and blinded by the devil that I couldn't and didn't accept that truth about myself. I was in denial, which I found to be a zone of lies and self-deception. I call it "the Enemy zone" or "the gone zone." It was a mind-blowing thought that God had showed up in the same room where I'd spent countless times fussing and cussing with someone I'd been in a relationship with for fifteen years. So many ugly and sinful things had taken place in this very room: drunkenness, fornication, blackouts, and lots of my getting high by myself because I didn't want to be around others when I was using it. I never imagined that He would come to such a dark place and that He would reach down so low to get someone like me out of a pit of hell. And yet He showed up. I know that if He did it for someone as nothing as I was, then it is easy for Him to do it for you or someone you know and care about.

Now, let me tell you just how He showed up and showed Himself to be an able, mighty, and miracle-working God after coming to my house that day.

Two weeks earlier, I walked into my bedroom to do what I had gone in there to do, when somehow my television was set to a religious channel. On the screen was a pastor from a church in Atlanta, Georgia. He was calling out a scripture, which was 1 Peter 5:7 from the King James Bible. He said, "God is speaking to you right now, and He is saying, cast all your care on Him for He cares for you."

I turned and looked over at the television, waved him off with my hand, and said, "Yeah, right, God ain't thinking about me with my little ugly, drunken stinking behind." Then I reached down to the nightstand and went on with what I had come to do in the first place, which was to take a couple of hits of cocaine, pour me a drink of cognac, and light a cigarette. I turned off the television and walked out of the room.

I had read scripture in the past, before I became a backslider, that said, "Keep thy heart with all diligence; for out of it are the issues of life" (Proverbs 4:23 KJV). Even though I had read this scripture, I didn't understand it meant that I was to be careful what I allowed to enter my spirit by what I looked at through my eye gate, what I received by listening to or heard through my ear gate and believed, and what I bring about by speaking out of my mouth (words). These are the gates you open for things to enter inside you, and whether it be positive or negative, it will manifest in some way or another. And if you speak it out of your mouth, then your words have the power to create the very thing that you spoke, if you believe in your heart what you said. "Not that which goeth into the mouth defileth a man; but that which cometh out of the mouth, this defileth a man (Matthew 15:11 KJV).

I say this because it was only two weeks after seeing and hearing that Pastor on television that I took it in through my eyes and ears, and this thing came back up in my spirit. I had gone into the bathroom and was standing in front of the mirror looking at myself, but I could not recognize myself—the image staring back at me looked like a monster. It was me, but it wasn't me. It was me combined with the demons that were inside me.

So, I started to talk to it—the monster. I looked right into its glassy, gazing, bloodshot eyes, and I said, "You ugly blankety-blank, with your filthy stinking blankety-blank and your blankety-blank self! You have taken all the years of my life that you're gonna take from me. Today I'm taking my life back. You gotta go. Get out of my life."

Just look at the words that were coming out of my mouth! Now, at that moment I had no clue as to how I was going to make that happen. I just knew that out of nowhere an unfamiliar and new kind of courage and strength had risen inside me that I never had before. I started crying and wiping tears from my eyes over and over. After wiping the tears, I threw the tissue at the image in the mirror, and I never looked back.

I walked out of the bathroom and up the hallway. It was a shotgun-style house where you could see the back door from the front door, straight down the hallway and outside the house. As I entered the living room, a feeling came over me suddenly and took control of me. I saw my hands going up in the air, but it was not I that had raised them up—it was more like someone else had just taken hold of them and put them up for me. You know how in the old western movies the cowboy would get a gun drawn on him suddenly and unexpectedly, so that he doesn't have time to draw back? So, he just puts his hands up in the air, surrenders, and gives up the fight. That's what I must have looked like while standing there in the middle of my living room. I looked up at my hands and asked myself, why are my hands up in the air like this? I had to ask because as an addict and alcoholic who had been oppressed by Satan for such a long time, I never really looked up far—there was so much weight on me from guilt, shame, depression, sadness, anger, frustration, confusion, fear, defeat, pain, and everything that was negative in my life, everything that was so heavy, that looking up itself was too painful.

Looking at my hands, being that they were already in the air, caused me to see past my fingertips, at which point my eyes became fixed on the ceiling. Now, I've been in a Baptist church almost all of my life, I thought, and I don't even know God personally for myself, but I feel that right now something is happening here, and it is making me want to strip off all my foolishness and pride to try and get nakedly honest before Him. I was thinking that I needed to tell God about my present truths; I mean, just open my heart to Him and not hold back anything. So, I started to talk to Him.

I said, "God, I don't know You, and I don't know who You are. My grandmother knew You, and my mother knew You, but I don't know You. I know about You, but I would like to know You for myself. My grandmother told me that You hear and see all things and that You know all things and that You are a good God. I believe there is a God, but I don't even know if You hear me right now, nor am I for sure that You really are real. But if You are real, then I need You to show me today—not tomorrow, not next week or next month, but I need You to show me today, right now. I need You to take away the alcohol, drugs, and cigarettes and get me out of this fifteen-year-old big black hole that I have dug for myself and can't get out of."

I told God, "I like getting high, and I like drinking the alcohol, but it is killing me, and I know it. So, I need and want You to take it away from me." I said to God again, "I believe there is a God, but I've been thinking that you're waaay out in space somewhere afar off. "So, if what my grandmother said was true, then You have seen me trying for the past three years to get out of this big black hole that I've dug for myself. You've seen me even after deciding that I had enough willpower to overcome this thing. Then You've looked at me as my will and I continued getting high together for the past three years. It was not enough for me to win. I needed something bigger and stronger than willpower and me."

So, I said to God, "I know you didn't create me just to come on your earth, suck up Your air, and burn up my brain cells getting high. There's got to be more to life than this, so please, God, if You'll take it away, clean me up from the inside out, make me the person that You created me to be, 'cause I don't know how to be that unless You show me. Then I'll tell somebody. Now God, I'm doing what Your man of God that I saw on television the other day told me to do. I'm casting all my cares on You for I believe that You care for me."

I had no clue what "casting your care" really looked like or meant, and remember, I had been around church folk practically all my life but was still clueless, because without the Holy Spirit they were clueless and powerless too. So, I just went with what casting a care might look like to me at the time. I started throwing up my hands to the ceiling, as if I was throwing a large beach ball to God up above my head. I said to God, "Here are the drugs, cocaine, and weed; I'm casting that on You. Here is the alcohol bottle; I'm casting that on You too."

By the second round of casting things that I'd been carrying, I noticed that I was starting to feel as if some weights were being lifted off my shoulders. I began to feel lighter and freer from that stuff that I had cast already. So, I became a casting fool. I said, "Here are the cigarettes, God; I'm casting them on You. Here are the bills in this house; I'm casting them too."

Then I said, "Here is my man, and here are my

children." I only had one small child at home at that time; one was an adult and in her own place in Atlanta. "Now God," I said, "It's no longer my problem. It's Yours because I've done what Your man of God instructed me to do. I've cast all my care on You, and now I'm opening my heart to invite You to come into my heart and give me Your Holy Spirit so that I may be able to live for You."

At this point, after about a good three to five seconds, or so it seemed, I started to feel some type of activity down in my belly, like a little bit of a quivering, so I looked down at my belly to see what was going on. I had never felt anything like that before, and when I saw that I was breathing as usual, I looked back up toward God and then back down at my belly, then back up toward God again, and I asked, "Is that You?"

It's kind of funny now, but at the time nothing about it was funny. After asking that question, suddenly tears just started streaming down my face. There was such a peace that came over me, as if someone had thrown a huge comforter or a great big room-size blanket of peace over me and my living room. And because I had never experienced that kind of peace, it was at that very moment I realized Jesus Himself, the Prince of Peace, had personally come for me.

> For unto us a child is born for unto us a son is given: and the government shall be upon his shoulder: and His name shall be called Wonderful, Counselor, The mighty God, The Everlasting Father, The Prince of Peace. (Isaiah 9:6 KJV)

The Prince of Peace Himself arrested me—not in a house of God, not in some church person's house, but in my house; the very place that I had been held captive in an invisible jail cell. He became the Master key to open that cell door and set me free, free from being controlled by the thoughts and or the strongholds which were all in my mind. Because the battle is between your ears.

You see, the devil, aka Satan, had me so bound and messed up in my mind that I could not even see the bars of my invisible jail cell. I was very much locked up, locked in, chained, bound, shackled, enslaved, and held hostage by the enemy and the disease called addiction. You see, the addiction was the stronghold of thoughts built by the enemy who was commander in chief to me in my soul—my mind, will, and emotions. The drug was my warden controlling me. I followed the orders of the commander in chief Satan and kept believing his lies. He told me when, where, and how to do things, even when to get up every day, only to start the vicious cycle all over again.

So, after having the blanket of peace thrown over me, the tears just started streaming down my face. I remember looking up yet again and saying to God, "Wow! You really are real, aren't You?" And when I said that the quivering activity going on in my belly started to speed up, and there was not a shadow of doubt in my mind that it was Jesus Himself in my house—Jesus had come to rescue and claim me as His very own.

After that I just lost it. It was as if someone had come into my house and poured a huge bucket of joy over my head, and it penetrated all the way inside to my brain and down into my heart and infected me. It looked like something you see at the football game when the winning team all ran over to the coach and poured the bucket of Gatorade on his head, because to me it felt as if I had won a victory, except it was not a game. In my real-life crisis, Jesus came, snatched me out of the hand of the devil, and rescued me from him. I was the walking dead, and when He came to my house, He resurrected me and gave me a new life much better than the one before. I was saved from real death, because there was a real devil trying to take me out, and the real Jesus stepped in right after my crying out to Him in a matter of minutes and delivered me in an instant, just like that. He wanted me to be free more than I wanted me to be free, so that once He got me out, He could clean me up, because that's how much He loves us.

And He loves you too, so much that He would send me back in to come after you, to let you know to call on Him so you can be set free too. He wants you because you have lost your identity just as I had, and He wants to show you who you truly are and who He created you to be in and to this world. He has a great plan already in place waiting for you. You're not waiting on Him; He's waiting on you.

So go ahead anytime, turn off your cell phone, and go to the throne of grace and make the call. Just say "Jesus!" Just look up, open your heart, and speak up. And if this message is not for you, then it is for someone you know, love, and care about. So please pass this word on to them!

2

BEFORE THAT MOMENT, I HAD NEVER KNOWN THE true meaning of joy. I had only experienced happiness—a happiness that was temporary and conditional, depending on situations and circumstances. Think about it: you have experienced happiness before, but it was only because something good had happened. Then suddenly, someone said or did something to you, and you lost your happiness—it went right out the window because of the circumstance or situation that occurred. Happiness is temporary, but joy remains. As written in John 15:11 (KJV), "These things have I spoken unto you, that my joy might remain in you, and that your joy might be full." This is the kind of joy that only comes from Jesus Christ the Lord. He gives us a peace that the world cannot produce:

> Peace I leave with you, my peace I give unto you: not as the world giveth, give I unto you. Let not your heart be troubled, neither let it be afraid. (John 14:27 KJV)

So, with all this excitement and deliverance taking place, I said to God, "Man, you are so awesome!" And so, it was on. I was like a bull coming out of a gate just opened wide. I ran around the house as if I had lost my mind. It's funny now; I realize that I had lost my mind and had gained the mind of Christ when I opened my heart to Him and invited Him and the Holy Spirit to come in and have His way with me and in me. I felt that I was the happiest and most joyful person on the earth that day. I knew that God had come and was arresting me to set me free for His Kingdom's purpose for my life. He was doing for me what I had not been able nor ever would be able to do for myself, even with all my willpower.

As I was running around like crazy, thanking and praising God for what He was doing in me and to me, suddenly I was stopped in my tracks. Just as joy had come like that bucket of Gatorade, it was as if someone now poured a bucket of fear over me. I stood there in my tracks, frozen with fear; then I heard a still, small voice say: "God hath not given us the spirit of fear; but of power, and of love, and of a sound mind" (2 Timothy1:7 KJV). I remembered that I had heard those words spoken as scripture before, either in Sunday school or in Bible study. So, in the middle of talking to the Creator of the universe, I stopped and addressed the devil who was trying to stop me from believing and receiving my deliverance from God.

"Oh, hell no, devil," I said to him, "you are not going to stop me from getting out of this jail cell today. My Lord has come for me, and I'm going with God."

So, I raised my arms high in the air in a crisscross,

swung them down toward the floor as hard as I could, and said to Satan, "Get out of my house right now in Jesus's name." As soon as I said that I felt something break loose in front of me, like a wall of bricks that came crumbling down, and I literally felt them as they fell and hit the floor on and in front of my feet. I went ballistic, way out there in the supernatural in my mind and my actions. I started to praise God three times as much as before. I felt as though I had become another person, and while I knew I was the same person, I was not the same on the inside. I then said to God, "I believe that You are taking away the alcohol and drugs from me, so bring it on God. Do whatever You have to do."

It was only God, Satan, and me together in my living room that day. It was war right before my eyes.

It was only a short while afterward that I was prompted by the Holy Spirit to look at the time. I saw that it was time to go pick up Makayla, my little girl from the daycare. I couldn't stop the tears of joy from flowing, but I had to go because the daycare she attended had a rule that if you hadn't picked your child up by 6:00 p.m., there would be a charge of five dollars and a dollar per minute after that. So, in my effort to leave, I ran into the bathroom, grabbed a facecloth, threw it across my shoulder, then grabbed my purse and keys and started towards the front door.

It was then I heard the voice of Satan say, "You better not go out that door because you are looking and acting like a fool, and the neighbors are going to be laughing at you and talking about you."

And I said to him, "Well, I don't care. They're just

gonna have to talk 'cause I'm going. Now go from here in Jesus's name."

I can't honestly tell you whether the neighbors even saw me because I can't remember even looking up at them. Two of the neighbors' houses directly across the street from me were occupied by close relatives who were usually sitting out on their porches. So now I'm in my car and I'm backing out of the driveway. I put the car in reverse and said to God, "You're gonna have to drive this car because I'm too drunk to drive it." And I felt as if God was saying, "I know, and I've got you, so no matter what, it's all right. Just flow with me."

By this time, I fully believed I was in some kind of metamorphosis. I was enroute to the daycare, without much control over what was going on. I was still talking to Jesus and blown away by His visiting somebody like me in the first place. I was so gone, but I was gone in the God zone, the victory zone, taken out of myself. I was beating on the steering wheel and the dashboard, saying to Him, "I can't believe this day! I can't believe You really are real. Thank You for coming. Thank You for showing me that You really are real. You are so awesome to me."

Then I would say, "God, stop it," and yet in the same breath I'd say, "No, God, no, no, no. Don't stop it. This is what I've been wanting and praying for, so if You're taking away the drugs and alcohol and cleaning me up, then just keep on doing what You're doing for me. I've asked You for it, so let me have all of it. Fill me with Your Holy Spirit!" Then I would go from crying to laughing, and from laughing right back to crying. I was totally out of control.

I was only a couple of blocks away from the daycare when it came to me that these people were not going to let me sign out my baby with me behaving in this manner. They would probably call the police, and the police would have someone from social services come and take my child away in their custody because I was drunk. Drunk in the Holy Ghost! I had been drinking that new wine, Spiritual wine, that came down from Heaven.

As I sat at the last red light before arriving at the daycare, I said to God, "God, I don't want You to stop what You're doing in me, because I believe you are taking away the drugs and alcohol and rescuing me. But I've got to go inside and get my child out, so I just need You to hold up what You're doing just long enough for me to go inside, sign her out, and get back in the car. Then You can start back up again right where You left off."

All at once, and I mean suddenly, it was as if there was a lot of water in my belly, and it got held up or pushed back in a holding position. Then I saw a picture in my mind of a movie that I had seen where the waters were being held up as they were at the Red Sea with Moses and the slaves of Egypt in The Ten Commandments. Just like that, everything stopped. I looked up to God and said, "Man, You're so awesome. I didn't know You did stuff like this. Woo-hoo! If I'd known you did stuff like this, I would have come to You a long time ago. Wow!"

I slowly eased on up the road in a state of shock and was just amazed. I was totally out of myself and in awe of God. As I entered the parking lot and turned off the car, I looked into the rearview mirror to try and fix myself and regain a reasonable amount of composure so I could go inside to get Makayla. Sure enough, they let me sign her out. But as soon as we got on the other side of the door, she looked up at me as I held her hand and asked, "Mommy, why are you so happy today?"

I remember thinking that as cool as I was trying to be and look, this baby could see that something was different about her mom. And I answered by saying, "Mommy is happy because God is here. Now let's just get in the car."

"Well, I want to be happy too," she said.

"OK, you can be happy too. Come on, let's get in the car." My next thought was that I'd better hurry up and get back in the car because I didn't know what God might do next, being I don't know Him well yet.

We got in the car, and I got her strapped into her car seat. I started out of the parking lot, and as soon as I was able to straighten the steering wheel, it was as if God had let go of the waters that He had held up in my belly, just as at the Red Sea where He had been holding back the waters for them to pass through. God heard me and did exactly as I had asked of Him. He held up everything until I could get my child out, and then He picked back up right where He left off. God was so amazing I'll never forget it as long as I live. Everything started rushing in on me again right where it had stopped so that I could go into the daycare.

By then I was just done. I said, "God, I don't know who I'm going to tell about this, but I gotta tell somebody. I am gonna tell what You have done for me, in me, and to me." Then I thought, who's gonna believe me? Just as I didn't know He made personal encounters; nobody I knew had ever mentioned anything like that to me. So, I didn't know who I could tell and not have them think that I had lost my mind.

But that day, He became my one true and living God. He became as real to me as my children. I know He is alive because He visited me, and I can feel Him inside me. He speaks to me, and He touches me. Yes, He is real! Just as real as the air I breathe. I now know this for myself, for I am yet another witness who has been captivated and infected by Him and His Word.

From that day, I knew that I had to do whatever it took to get to know Him for myself and not to just pretend I know Him like a regular churchgoer.

When God came to me and led me out of my invisible jail cell, I had been in a backslidden state for many years. I was living in sin with a man for fifteen years; I believed and felt that it was the best I could do, the best I could have in my life. I thought it would never get any better for me, so I had settled and never looked forward to any expectation of a better future for myself. I had let the lie of the Enemy in my head, and it caused me to believe that I was not good enough, that I didn't deserve better. I had absolutely bought that costly lie.

AT THE TIME THAT HE DELIVERED ME, I WORKED night shift at a private hospital. The first thing I started to do was to come home every morning after work and take Makayla to daycare and return home. Makayla's father-Rico King-owned and ran his business and he would be gone by the time I would get back to the house. That was great because I would have the house all to myself with no distractions. I wanted to go after God with full force, so I turned off the television, radio, and ringer on the phone, then closed the blinds and immersed myself in the Word of God, the Bible. I also ordered a book titled God Chaser. I became relentless on the quest to learn of God and His character.

I felt that I had to fully get with Him and go His way, because my way was no longer working for me. I mean, I had plenty of years when sin was fun and felt good at the time. But that was when I thought I was calling the shots and didn't know that it was the devil in me that was really calling them. My sin cost me so much of myself that I ended up losing my identity during it all. The pain behind the sin was so great that it outweighed the pleasure, and that is when I was ready to get to know God.

So, as I moved on, there were mornings I would turn on the television and study with some bible teaching and preaching Pastors. I would always study with Pastors that taught in a practical way so that I had a clearer understanding of the word of God.

After the teachings and preachings had gone off, I would go in and close the door to the bedroom, kneel at the foot of my bed, and say to God, "Thank You for coming to show me that You are really real and for snatching me out of the hands of the Enemy and setting me free from the bondage of addiction." I would thank Him for the Holy Spirit that was living and working inside me to help me and show me things that I knew not of, like His Word said. I would thank Him for Jesus, who had taken my sins upon Himself and suffering; His shed blood on the cross; His death, burial, and resurrection just for me, a full-fledged sinner and a nobody. I told Him that if I had only known that He could and would get me out of my addiction, then I would have come to Him a long time ago. There is no way that I would have lived the lifestyle I was for so long, a life so beneath my privileges and without my godly benefits: "Blessed be the Lord, who daily loadeth us with benefits, even the God of our salvation. Selah" (Psalm 68:19 KJV). The word Selah means to pause and calmly think about what was just spoken.

I had been missing so much and didn't even realize it. So, I thought, even if I could muster up enough courage to talk to God, everybody that I had listened to said, "God don't listen to no drunken dopehead sinner," but that's not true 'cause I was hungover when He came for me. And

God is married to the backslider: "Turn, O backsliding children, saith the Lord; for I am married unto you: and will take you one of the city and two of a family, and I will bring you to Zion" (Jeremiah 3:14 KJV).

Keep in mind, too, that before God came for me, Makayla's father Rico and I were living together in sin, unmarried, and had been for several years. When we met, I was in the retail for men's clothing, and he was out shopping for a suit to wear to a big meeting his mother's church had once a year in the country. He said he took her every year and always bought her a new outfit and a new wig to wear. That's how he got my attention, and I must admit that I was impressed after spending about $400 on his attire and shoes, he asked if I would go with him to get his pants hemmed at the tailor shop, we used and then afterward to help him pick out a wig for his mother. I said yes. I wanted to be professional and helpful, being that he seemed kind and was also very generous with his tip after his purchase. I was interested in him.

After a couple of hours, he took me home, and we exchanged phone numbers when I got out of his car. He didn't come in but it was the beginning of a fifteen-year relationship. We started seeing each other, and it wasn't long before we had fallen in love and didn't want to be anywhere without the other. We would travel so frequently on the weekends that I had a special bag I kept packed and ready to go. After being together for about two years, he asked me to marry him, but for some reason or another, I could not say yes. Over the years, he bought four sets of wedding rings, but we never made it to the altar. Something inside me just wouldn't let me have peace about going forth in marriage with him.

Things were good until trust became an issue. We started to have a breakdown in communication. After seven years of this, we started a pattern of breaking up and getting back together again. By this time, everything had spiraled out of control. He had always drunk beer after work, but on the weekends, he would drink a lot more. To be fair, while he was drinking outside our home, I was at home drinking alcohol and getting high on cocaine, so by the time he got home, I would be good and high. We would go out to the clubs or to a shot house three or four nights a week, and he came home every night, so I never really could see where he would even have the time to cheat. We were good financially and great together sexually, but spiritually and emotionally we were bankrupt. Things had gotten so bad between us that we would start to argue within fifteen minutes of having sex. We had lost all sense of respect for each other. There was so much ugliness. Finally, we decided that we just needed to stop trying to make it work and go our separate ways.

Shortly after that, only about a week later, one of his aunts died. and we ended up arriving at the same time at her house, where the family was sitting up before the funeral. We were not together, but we were visiting the same house together, and none of the family members knew that it was over between us for good. No more getting back together like before!

While we were sitting there, though we were not sitting together, his cousin, who was dating my adult daughter

Mahogany, came up with the ideal of the four of us taking a trip to Disney World the weekend after the burial. So even though we had both decided to call it quits once and for all we said OK.

The weekend rolled around, and we headed to Tampa, Florida. On the way, we checked into a beautiful hotel to spend the night. We were tired, and there was enough time to stay overnight and go on to Disney World the next morning. We were in the room, talking about getting freshened up to go out for food, when suddenly I became irritated with him and everything he said and did. Even his voice became annoying to me. Then, as if that wasn't enough, I became so ill that I started throwing up. I felt horrible, as if I had gotten food poisoning. Something was going on; something was wrong with my stomach. I did not want to be touched by him, and I slept the whole night through.

The next morning, after getting up and showering I was OK until he started to talk to me. And then it was on with us disagreeing again. That's when we knew we were not about to make it to Disney World even after traveling that far. I felt so bad for Mahogany and her boyfriend not being able to go to Disney World. They didn't know we had called it off for the final time and were just a mess.

We ended up returning home, and I could hardly wait until Monday morning to make an appointment to see my doctor and find out what was going on with me. The only time I remember being sick enough to throw up was when I was pregnant with my first child twenty-two years earlier, but I quickly dismissed that thought. Before this all came about, my ob-gyn had told me I could not have any more children because of taking Depo-Provera shots for more than twelve years. He had informed me that this form of birth control was not to be taken for more than ten years because it could cause sterility. This was his medical opinion, anyway.

So, unsuspecting, I went to see my family practice physician, not my ob-gyn, to get checked out and see if I had food poisoning or just what the matter was with me. The doctor ordered tests, and when the results came back, the nurse called me into the room to go over them. "Ms. Johnson," she said, "there is nothing wrong with you, and you're not sick. You're just pregnant."

Well, I immediately asked the craziest question I could have asked. "How did that happen?" I asked in shock. She looked at me as if she wanted to ask, "Do you really need me to answer that?"

I started crying because I just couldn't believe it. I had been told that it was impossible for me to have another baby. My only child at the time was twenty-two years old, with two kids of her own, living in her own apartment, and about to graduate from college. And my point to you is, yes, listen to what your doctor has to say, but you absolutely cannot take the findings of a doctor's report as the final truth. They have facts and can show them to you on paper or on the X-rays or whatever, but the Word of God is the truth and has the power to turn a fact into a lie. The doctor said I could not get pregnant and have any more babies because of the birth control that I had used, but the truth that is the Word of the Lord said, "But he was wounded for our transgressions, he was bruised for our iniquities: the chastisement of our peace was upon him; and with his stripes we are healed." (Isaiah 53:5 KJV).

The main thing I was crying about was that I had arrived at a place in my life where I made a final decision never to go back into the poisonous relationship I had been in and out of for seven years, and now, out of all the things that could have happened, I was pregnant. Oh my God!

After a couple of days of thinking about what to do about this situation and how it came up at the worst possible time, I called Rico to talk. We talked about the baby and decided that even though things were not good between us anymore, we still cared about each other, and our baby was worth our efforts to try to get it together.

We made an appointment to go to family counseling and started seeing a therapist together. Even though we agreed to try harder, things still were not where they should have been, but the baby came, and we were OK. Her name was Makayla. We loved our baby girl so much and spent lots of time together bonding with her. We were proud parents, and she was our beautiful baby.

But even though Makayla meant the world to us, there were still plenty of unresolved issues between us. I just wanted to get out of it and was desperate to have peace in my life.

FINALLY, I DECIDED THAT I WAS GOING TO LEAVE RICO and our beautiful house. I was so miserable that I started to pack certain items and waited for the right opportunity to bring in the moving truck and get out of there.

And God had already made a way out of no way. I was able to move into a house that my great-aunt had lived in. It was built shotgun style, as I mentioned before, where you could look from the front door straight down the hallway and see the back door. It had two bedrooms, a living room, a dining room, a bathroom, and a kitchen. It was beautiful to me, though, because Makayla and I had escaped the madness and constant state of chaos that we had experienced while living with Rico.

When I left Rico, I didn't have a car of my own, so I took one of his four cars, hoping that he wouldn't find me before I could get one of my own. But after a couple of months, with the help of one of my relatives he did find me.

The truth, we were just spiritually illiterate. Neither of us had a clue that the devil had been busy operating in our lives, trying to destroy not only our relationship and family but us as individuals. We were so busy doing things our way that we didn't recognize that God had a plan for each of our lives. So, we started communicating again, but only over the phone, for the next couple of months. By then, I had hit a rough patch financially, and it had started to look like I couldn't do it on my own. I had to keep my child with the material things she needed while still trying to support my use of cigarettes, drugs, and alcohol. Keeping everything running in the house as well as making the rent, it had become overwhelming.

After trying on my own for three months, I gave in to him and let him move in with us. I felt I needed his help, and after all, he was the father of my child and I had no right to take her father away from her—and I still loved him, in a strange and sick way. All of this was just a bunch of excuses I made up. Excuses are crutches: they support you in being crippled. And if your mind is crippled, then your life is crippled. However a person lets their mind think will determine how they are in their life. I was giving up only three months after leaving him simply because I was still operating without God leading and guiding me. I was still using the drugs and alcohol, I was still lazy from using, I was still feeling sorry for myself while on a pity pot, and I still wanted things done my way, which was the bottom line: "simply stupid."

So even though I didn't like what he had become, I took him back—and opened the door for the enemy to do even more harm to me and my child mentally, emotionally, physically, and spiritually in ways that could scar us. The enemy often uses the ones you're closest to.

After we got back together, it was only a little while before the same unresolved issues resurfaced.

At this point, I decided to go back to work. I worked the night shift, where I was very content because I didn't have to be at home with him. Rico was committed to coming home every night to keep Makayla during this time, and she was happy with him.

As time went on, I started to notice that I did not want to go out with him anymore to the places we used to go. Even when we went back to our favorite places, we most enjoyed with each other, I just was not happy at all. Nothing was the same. He became more filled with anger and discontent, and so did I. We were living together for the sake of Makayla.

I didn't realize it, but God had His hand on my life and was dealing with me even then. Everything started to shift. I was drinking and drugging but no longer getting much pleasure out of it. I was being with Rico sexually but no longer getting much pleasure out of it. I hated myself, and I hated my life no matter what we did to try to make it better. We would pack and go out of town like we used to and stay in great hotels, but it didn't change anything. It seemed like an impossible and hopeless situation. I had no clue at the time that a divine interruption of God was happening.

Then I started experiencing spiritual encounters. The first one happened one day after I had laid down to take a nap. I was probably in the first stage of sleep when suddenly I felt like something was walking across my king-size bed. My eyes were closed, and I could not open them, but I could sense the presence of four demons. Two of them came up to my head; one covered my mouth, and the other covered my nose, trying to suffocate me. I could not breathe. I was trying to shake them loose by moving my head from side to side, and when I couldn't, I started to call on the name of Jesus as loud and as hard as I could, given that my mouth was bound. That's when they turned me loose, and I was able to open my eyes and see them as they ran across my bed and back out of the bedroom. I couldn't believe it, but I had to—it happened to me, and I saw it with my own eyes. At that time, I was too disconnected from God to really understand why this was happening and just what was going on.

A couple of days later, the thought came to me that this thing had happened because of the sin in the house. I had been raised by my mother and my grandmother and taught that to be living with a person and having sex without being married to them was a sin in the eyes of God—fornication. Our bed was defiled. Still, I continued living my life as I had been.

About three months later, I experienced a second spiritual encounter. I woke up from a blackout on the loveseat in the living room, at home alone that day because my baby girl had gone to Atlanta to spend the weekend with her big sister Mahogany. Lying there, I looked over toward the double windows and saw a big black silhouette in the form of a man stepping through the window—without my window being opened. Really, he just stepped through the window. I became so afraid as he started walking towards me and came around the side of the loveseat where I was lying flat on my back. He stood right over my head, looking down in my face, and I couldn't even lift a finger to move. The fear was so strong that it paralyzed me. I didn't know what to do, so I closed my eyes and said, "God, if You don't let him take me this time, I promise I will never drink this much alcohol again." I was still too addicted and crazy to tell God that I would quit; I just said I wouldn't drink that much again.

What a merciful God He is that after I talked like that to Him, He did not let whatever that thing was have its way with me. I've tried to figure out what it was: maybe some kind of spirit of death. Even when I was in such a low state in my life, God loved me and protected me as I was His very own and wouldn't let go of me, for He had a plan and there was yet a purpose for even a mess like me. And while I continued in this sick lifestyle for a time, I never drank that amount of alcohol again, as I said to Him I wouldn't, even while using cocaine and smoking cigarettes. Somehow in my twisted thinking I still had a certain amount of fear about lying to God, although the addiction kept its grip on me. I continued using it to cope with my life as it was instead of waking up to the reality of the danger and defeat of it all.

The thing is, I and anyone else should be able to see just how crazy it is and how much we need help when we continuously want more of the very thing that has taken our lives hostage and brought it to a standstill. But you've gotta want to do better, no matter what, before you do better.

Now, the third encounter happened on a Saturday when Rico was out on the construction site working on a job. He was so excited that he had won the bid by just a few dollars. It was a huge contract, and I was excited about it too, so I decided that while he was out working, I was going to celebrate because of the money that was on the way to the house.

I fed Makayla some breakfast, then proceeded to clean the house. After the house cleaning, it started to rain. I decided to put on some oxtails and let them cook, and since it was raining and I didn't want or need to go out of the house for anything, I could use cocaine and alcohol as my drug of choice to celebrate such a great occasion and just stay in the house and chill. Makayla was good, her room filled with more than enough toys for her to play with, so I was good also.

I had been high when I went to bed the night before, so my system already had plenty in it the next morning, and it didn't take a whole lot to put me down. I ended up in a blackout. When I woke up from it, I discovered that my house was engulfed with smoke from the oxtails burning on the stove. All I could think to do was roll over off the loveseat onto the floor and crawl through the dining room to the kitchen. I had to turn off that stove!

But when I got to the stove and grabbed the pot to remove it from the burner to my surprise the stove had already been turned off. I had no time to think about how it would be turned off, because I needed to open the back door to try and let some of the smoke out quickly. I was so scared, praying, God, please let my little girl be OK.

I finally made it to her bedroom. To my surprise, she was on her knees calmly playing pushing a toy car that my grandson had left there during his last visit. The smoke was hovering just over and above her head and back. I grabbed her and ran out the back door, crying tears of joy and thanking God for her being alive and for protecting her from smoke inhalation by keeping her preoccupied on the floor, pushing that car around. It appeared that the Lord had sheltered her body and her mind so well that she didn't even question me even with my being in such a frantic state.

After being kept and protected by God through all of this, I still chose to continue using the drugs and alcohol, until the time came where I became so weighed down with pain that I had to look up, open up, and speak up, as the Pastor on the television had instructed me to. And that was the day of my personal encounter with God Himself, when He came and arrested me and set me free from the bondage of Satan in my house, my very own invisible prison cell, for His plan and purpose for my life and for His glory.

After He arrested me, I became goal oriented. Every weekday morning for about twelve and a half months, I established a routine of continuously seeking Him. I wanted to know Him for myself after seeing for myself that He was very real and very alive. After studying the Word of God in my Bible daily with the pastors I mentioned earlier, I would usually play praise and worship music, and then move from praise to prayer. He would meet with me there every morning. My favorite time of seeking Him was from 9 a.m. to 11 a.m. or sometimes until noon—it depended on what He wanted to do to me, in me, and with me on that day.

Oh, He is a mind blower and will never cease to amaze you. Some days after He did what He did to me, I could hardly wait to seek Him again the next day, for I didn't know what He was going to do the next time. Each time with Him became more and more exciting, as if each time would outweigh or be better and stronger than the last. He is full of mystery and wonder like no other you've ever encountered in your life. No other lover can do you like He can. He'll show you when you go after Him wholeheartedly.

Hebrews 11:1, 6 (NIV) says,

> Now faith is confidence in what we hope for and assurance about what we do not see ... And without faith it is impossible to please God, because anyone who comes to Him must believe that He exists and that He rewards those who earnestly seek Him.

I remember the first time He allowed me to get into His presence without music playing but just with my heart, for I was falling in love with Him. One time in the beginning when He put His hand on my back and gently leaned me forward and over into a bowed-down position, teaching me how to revere and worship Him. He made me come to know His presence without a doubt.

5

AFTER THE FIRST COUPLE OF MONTHS OF SEEKING Him, I started to hear the Christian people on television say, "God wants you to pray in the spirit." I did not yet have that heavenly language, even though it was something I desired. I wanted to speak with other tongues so much that I told God, "You said that You would give me the desires of my heart; then why can't I speak in tongues, because I desire it?" Well, He never said a word. He had mercy towards me for I was only an infant in Him and He knew I was spiritually immature. I only knew what religious folk looked and acted like—church folk. So, I just kept on asking for certain spiritual gifts in prayer and believing by faith that one day I would have what I had asked God for.

> Therefore, I say unto you, whatsoever things
> ye desire, when you pray, believe that you
> receive them, and ye shall have them. (Mark
> 11:24 KJV)

I did not know at the time that faith is always now; the moment that you believe it, receive it, and take that word by faith, you have it right then. You might not see the manifestation of it right away, but it is on the way for sure.

Now, it was about seven months later when the Lord led me to Atlanta for a healing crusade. The spirit was so high there that at one point I truly felt that God was walking toward me. I sensed His presence so strongly because I had learned what it felt like when He was near to me. So, I just opened my mouth and said, "God, I know you're here. Don't You pass me by!" At that very instant, I began to reach up and praise Him, saying, "Hallelujah!" It was as if He got to my row then reached over to me and took control of my tongue. Right then and there, I was given God's heavenly prayer language, and I have been speaking in tongues ever since that night.

That night I also learned that God would turn anywhere into His heavenly place where His will is being done on earth as it is in heaven. When I left that place, I not only was speaking in tongues but had such a powerful touch from God that it left me with a limp, as if my hip was almost out of the socket; I was suddenly crippled but with joy and excitement. When I look back on it, I'm reminded of the story in the Bible of Jacob wrestling with the angel and how his hip was put out of joint. I was so elated to be crippled by God's powerful touch that I didn't even have a thought whether I would remain that way—I was just ecstatically happy that I had received His heavenly prayer language and his personal touch. I had no shame about being unable to walk correctly as I had when I came in or to stop speaking in tongues.

When we went to a restaurant to get some dinner, I

couldn't order my food nor stop speaking in tongues long enough to eat. Rico looked at me like will you just cut it out? But I couldn't stop it, and we had to get a takeout tray so I could get out of there and back to the hotel room. It was all well with me because I had been given my desire to speak in tongues, and I had once again been touched by the Almighty God for real. I wished that everyone could feel what I was feeling—an overload of joy! That is an experience I will never forget as long as I live.

The next thing I confronted was the condition of my health and what shape I was in physically. There was a good possibility that my liver had been messed up with cirrhosis and my stomach full of cancer. I had used the drugs and alcohol and smoked cigarettes for a long time without eating and taking care of myself, and I had not gone to a doctor for any kind of checkup or physical in several years. So, I scheduled an appointment for a complete physical exam, including a pap smear.

While waiting for my appointment to roll around I decided to study the Bible (Basic Instructions Before Leaving Earth) on a particular topic: I wanted to know the will of God for my life. So, I went to the back of my Bible, which had a section of commentary by topic which all Bibles do not have, looked up God's will, and wrote down all the scriptures listed under God's will. I never knew that God's will would be so many things. I just thought it would be one big thing, but He wants more for us than we want for ourselves. One of the scriptures I looked up was 3 John 1:2, where I found out that it was God's will for me to be healed and prosper and be in health in my body and in my mind. So before going any further, I started to pray to God about what I had read in His Word.

Meanwhile, I had gone to the doctor and was waiting for my test results. All of them came back clean, except one. I was diagnosed with high blood pressure and was given a prescription to start medication immediately to help control it. This was when I really started to not only believe but know that God's hand had been on my life long before my personal encounter with Him, and that the devil had been trying to kill me for real.

The reality of the Enemy trying to kill me took me back in time to when I was a little girl. I had a stepfather who would babysit my brother and me while my mother was at work. My brother didn't care for our stepdad very much, so he stayed outside playing a lot or doing something with my grandfather, who lived right around the corner. One day, a lady friend of my mom and stepfather came over to visit him while my mother was at work. They were drinking something called "stump liquor" and decided to give me some of it. Then they walked to the store around the corner from our house and had me walk with them. When we got inside the store, I sat down in the middle of the floor, intoxicated and sick. They picked me up and took me back home, and I heard them say, "We cannot call her mother because she is going to kill us for giving it to her." So, they laid me down in the bed until my mother got home and took me to the hospital so they could pump my stomach. The devil was already after me back then.

It also reminded me of other times in that same big scary house where I used to see visions of different people going down the hall in a wheelchair pushed by the same nurse in a white uniform, a white cap, white stockings, and white shoes. This vision frightened and affected me for years to come to the point that when I was pregnant and had gone into labor, I was afraid to sit in the wheelchair when taken to the hospital. The devil tried to mess up my mind when I was a little girl during a lot of days and nights; I was afraid of the dark because we were not allowed to sleep with any light on in the house.

For a time while I was in elementary school, there was an adult male neighbor that was a friend of the family who would come over every morning to make sure my brother and I got out in time for school, since my mother had to be at work. One morning he tried to touch me in a wrong way, but for some reason he was not able to do what he had in mind. Now I realize that it was the Almighty Father who wouldn't allow him to have his way. I told my mother, and he never came to our house again.

When I turned thirteen, I started working in the school cafeteria, loading dishes in the dishwasher. By the age of fourteen, I worked at a hospital as a switchboard operator through a schoolwork program. At fifteen I became pregnant and had to transfer to a school that only pregnant girls attended. After having Mahogany I was able to return to my regular high school where I graduated from at the age of sixteen. At that time, it was almost impossible to be hired before the age of eighteen. So, I just went to work with my mom and helped her for a little while. My mom wanted so much more for me that she allowed someone to give me some type of medication that should have terminated the pregnancy; instead, it just made me sick and caused me to have to go back and forth to the emergency room. I lost so much weight that I was too weak to walk on my own, but God would not let go of me even then.

After living through that and having my healthy baby girl Mahogany, I stayed home with her until I could get a job. I became interested in retail clothing sales, which led me into a variety of jobs, even some modeling. Later, I was hired as a dispatcher for the ambulance service at a hospital. So, I went back to school at the age of twenty and became a certified emergency medical technician and the first black female to drive the ambulance at that place. I was working twelve-hour shifts, so my mother kept my daughter Mahogany.

It was while I was working this job that the devil entered my life more determined than ever to take me out. My life started to take a downward spiral a couple of years later after becoming involved with a thirty-one-year-old married man named Hammer where I was headed for pain and disappointment in my life because the devil came in through this man to kill me. There was nothing that money could buy that Hammer wouldn't have given me, but he was too controlling. He was very possessive, jealous, and controlling, as if he himself was possessed and being controlled by something to control me. Slowly I started becoming whatever he was molding, shaping, and programming me to be. I ended up missing a period, went to see a doctor, and was told I was six weeks pregnant. The physician I had gone to informed me that he was going to discontinue delivering babies and referred me to another ob-gyn who would deliver. No problem.

I went to see the new ob-gyn a couple of weeks later. After examining me, he informed me that I was not pregnant but had a cist on my womb. He said that I didn't have to worry because he could take care of it by performing laser surgery without me having to be cut on with a knife. Then he said, "Before performing laser surgery on you, I would like to try and see if we can cause the cist to resolve itself" by a particular treatment that we're going to administer to you. I took his word at face value and believed and trusted him. At the time I truly believed everything that a doctor said was the truth.

I continued going back and forth to my appointments with him, and because my stomach was not growing or getting any bigger, I believed that I only had a cist on my womb. But after about ten months, I started to have pain. I went in to see him and informed him of what I was experiencing, and he just gave me pain meds and told me that he would see me in two weeks. After getting home and going to bed, I found that the pain became so excruciating that even after taking the pain meds, I ended up right back in his office the very next morning. He had his nurse order an ultrasound to be done on me at a hospital.

During the ultrasound, they found not one but two babies that were in me and not moving. They had stopped growing and died inside me from not receiving the proper prenatal care because of this physician's wrong diagnosis. But it was yet another time the Enemy was unable to kill me, and God kept me. The babies had been dead long enough to become septic in my body, and I would have died if God had allowed it.

After being in a relationship with Hammer for seven years of my life and breaking my family's heart into pieces, I was finally able to end the relationship. It hurt me in the most painful way, but I saw that he was never going to leave his wife and kids for me. It felt like I was dying. I knew that I had to get away from Hammer to have a better life and future with someone who was not married. I was so totally devastated after breaking away from Hammer that I think I went temporarily insane. I quit my job, cut off all my hair to hurt him (because he had loved my long hair), and moved to Florida with my Mahogany.

6

AFTER THE MOVE, MY DAUGHTER, NOW NINE YEARS old was transferred to the elementary school in the community where we lived, but she had a hard time making the adjustment and adapting to the change of environment. It was the first time she had ever been away from my mother for an extended time. So, after four months I arranged for my mother and aunt to come to Florida and pick her up along with a school transfer packet to take back to Georgia. I would drive back and forth to Georgia to visit and spend time with Mahogany every other weekend.

In Florida, I started working for a dentist who was one of the nicest professional people I had ever met. He hired me to be his receptionist and personal assistant. He introduced me to a world of professional proprietors who were his friends as well as his patients. While working for the dentist, I became involved with a Caucasian guy who was nice and good to me. Our relationship was good, but it only lasted about three months. He frightened me when he became persistent about wanting to do things like get married without us taking more time to get to know one another. He even wanted to take out an insurance policy on himself and make me the beneficiary. It just seemed too weird to me to be discussing something of that nature in such a short period of time. So, we broke up, and I later moved back to Georgia.

Shortly after moving back home, I became involved in a relationship with Bassett, someone from my old neighborhood I knew of but hadn't really known personally. This was the individual who introduced me to powder cocaine. Before becoming involved with him, I had only used pot and alcohol occasionally. After trying this drug for the first time and using it on the weekends, my life really started to change—not just my persona, but my life. After being in a relationship with him for five years, I saw he was slowly losing his sense of responsibility and I was losing respect for him, so I released him and let him go. I couldn't go any further with him even though I still loved him.

Even though the relationship ended, the habit of using did not end with it. I was on my own to get it, but somehow, I had decided in my mind and heart that I would not become a prostitute no matter what. The one thing I said to myself was, I'll never spend my own money on this stuff; if no one will buy it for me, then I just won't have it. And yeah, right, self-deception; what a lie that was. So, after a short period of spending my own money on the stuff, I decided to become involved with a drug dealer who dealt in weight named Big John. Now I'm being supplied free drugs again, but in a much greater measure—two or three grams at a time, because he was away a lot working it and would never let me run out. Look at Satan coming at me harder than ever now to take me out.

I was so caught up that I had no clue about the spiritual and natural danger I was in. But God, who rules and reigns over Satan, stepped in and caused me to see how possessive and dominating Big John was. Big John would leave and lock me up in the house so that I couldn't get out even if there had been a fire. I became afraid and more cautious. I was no longer comfortable with him. Big John was a business owner—he owned and managed a popular band. He had me travel with him when they had to perform out of town or out of state on the weekends. I was getting high more than ever. I was entertaining company and had people over on a regular basis, playing cards and partying at my house. But Big John had become so possessive and crazy that I just couldn't take it anymore, so I ended the relationship.

I decided that I was not going to get involved in another relationship; instead, I would just be a friend with guys. I started spending my own money on alcohol, cigarettes, and cocaine again. But it was nowhere close to the amount I had become used to, so I was trying to find ways to wean myself off from it. No such thing, but I was able to slow down, and I only used it at night. I continued this way for a while.

And here is why I know now that God always has a plan for our lives, even when we have no clue. One day out of nowhere, my daughter Mahogany came to me and said, "Mama, I found you a job in the newspaper ads, and I have already scheduled an interview for you to go on next week." By the hand of God that used her, she took the initiative to pretend to be me over the telephone (we do sound very much alike). At that time, I had been out of work for a while and had not been thinking about going back into the work force at all. To God be the glory for using Mahogany to get me back into society and the workplace.

Now you will recall that I had been studying the Bible and had looked up scriptures on God's will for my life. The next topic I started to study was fear. I was walking around so scared of everything, especially the devil, because Rico and I were living in sin. It kept me feeling like something or someone was always watching and following me. Once when I was in my living room trying to pray the best I knew how, something started jumping up and down on the floor furnace in my hallway, about four feet from where I was kneeling to pray. I jumped up, looked at the floor furnace, and became frozen in my tracks. I thought, Rico is at work, it's raining so hard outside, everyone is at work, so whose house can I go to right now?

Then it hit me: I didn't have to leave my house because I'm scared of the devil. But the devil needed to leave because he didn't pay any bills there. So, there I was. After being born again for real, I decided that I'm not leaving. While afraid I walked to my refrigerator, pulled down the paper on which I had written some Bible verses concerning fear that another Pastor had taught on, and started back to the living room. As I was walking back, the fear increased. I was shaking and trembling like the scarecrow in the Wizard of Oz. Once I was back in the living room, I looked in the direction of the devil and stood there and said to him, "You can't stay here, devil. Only one of us can stay, and since you don't pay any bills here, that means you gotta go."

Then I started reading the scriptures off that paper to him.

"Greater is He that is in me than he that is in the world.'

"I can do all things through Christ which strengthens me.'

"I am the head and not the tail; I am above only and never beneath.'

"I'm blessed in the city; I'm blessed in the field. I'm blessed in my going out, I'm blessed in my coming in.'

"I'm more than a conqueror through Christ Jesus.

"I'm not afraid of the devil, 'because greater is He that is in me than he that is in the world.'†

"Now get out of my house and take the rest of 'em with you!"

I ran to the door and quickly opened it, shouting, "Get out now!" I looked back and didn't see anything, but I felt it there, so I said, "Yeah, you are going too. Come on, you've gotta go."

After that I felt some relief, as if something had shifted either in my house or in me, or both. I knew that something supernatural happened after those words came out of my mouth because the atmosphere suddenly felt better.

---

† Adapted from 1 John 4:4; Philippians 4:13; Deuteronomy 28:13; Deuteronomy 28:3, 6; Romans 8:37.

As these encounters went on, I remained in a relationship with Rico. For years, I had been hanging on for the sake of our daughter, whom we both loved dearly. I did not want to see her hurt because we couldn't get it together.

I spent a lot of time trying to get Rico to come over to the other side with me by going to church together and reading the Bible. Every now and again, he would show up to Bible study, but only to appease me. We even went to a couple of healing crusades together, and at one God healed him from bleeding ulcers.

Rico had already accepted Jesus as his Lord and Savior before I met him. The thing that drew me to him in the first place was his respect and love for his mother. But he was just not wanting to live a Christian lifestyle. He once commented, "God did not call me. He called you." And he was right. So, from that point on, I stopped trying to get him to change along with me.

After about two and a half years of waiting for him to get on board so we could finally be of one accord and blessed by God, one day I was walking down the hall and heard the voice of the Lord: "Cut him off!"

"But God," I said, "he pays all the bills. My check is to do what I please."

And God said: "Cut him off!"

"But God," I said again, "he is my provider."

And God said: "I am your Provider; trust Me."

"But I don't know how to trust You," I said.

And God said once more: "Trust Me."

"OK, God," I said, "but You're gonna have to teach me how to trust You. OK, now hold up!" Be very mindful of what you say to God, because often, what you say is what you get.

Well, nobody ever told me that once you surrender your life and submit unto His will for life, then you become like clay or putty in His hands to make, shape, and mold however and whatever pleases Him. He is the one who's in control. But the good news is, He always knows what's best for us. So just say yes to God and trust in His Word, no matter how long it takes for you to see God's plan come to pass. Give it up. Only He can make us who we were created and designed to be.

I had already left this man twice in my own strength, trying to find peace of mind. Each time I failed because I wasn't strong enough nor financially stable enough to stand alone without him, and my emotions kept overruling my decisions. I was too weak to fight because while I had been saved, I was not yet walking in the power of the Lord.

Now a couple of days after God had spoken to me about cutting Rico off, I was sitting on the front porch in the evening when he came home. I told him I needed to talk to him about something that had happened to me. I told him what God said, and he became very angry and said, "God didn't tell you that because God does not separate families." Rico ignored the fact that God had visited me.

Because Rico was a business owner, he was able to come home whenever he wanted. Sometimes, I would be sitting at the dining room table, studying the Bible, and he would come in and for his own selfish reasons just interrupt what I was doing to get closer to God. He would say things like, "I don't know what you're reading that Bible for, God don't know you." And I would respond by saying something like, "The blood of Jesus is against you, Satan," and he would leave the house in a rage, saying, "Stop speaking that voodoo to me. You are practicing witchcraft."

There were countless times when he came home just to start an argument, because he knew that he would find me trying to get closer to God. It was now clear to me that the closer to God I got, the stronger I became. Sometimes he would walk in on me in the bedroom and see me bowed down on my knees at the foot of the bed, praying to God, and he would begin calling my name to tell me to stop praying and just answer him. I would try to ignore him and continue to pray, but he would not stop calling me until I answered. He had no reverence for God, nor did he fear Him.

God also knew that Rico had begun sleeping with two guns under his pillow. When I questioned him about why the guns were there, he said he was hearing noises in the house, like someone running up and down the hallway when he was in bed. In seeing this I realized how much he was being set up by the devil because fear is one of the devil's greatest weapons that he uses to get us to react to his tactics. Again, the Enemy was trying to kill me by his hands, but God would not allow it.

One evening he agreed to sat down and talk it out. After he said all that, he wanted to say, which I took the time to listen, I told him that I had to move out of our bedroom with him and into our daughter's bedroom.

I also informed him that I would never have sex with him again. I moved out of our bedroom the next day, and our house became like living in heaven next door to hell.

7

WHEN OUR MAKAYLA WAS AT DAYCARE, RICO was at work, and I was spending my time learning things that God was revealing to me. It felt like God's Kingdom had come to me and His will was being done in my life on earth as it was in heaven.

At first, I thought I would be afraid of going to sleep in the house with the Enemy, but it really did feel like God was there in the house with me, protecting my child and me and teaching me how to trust in Him for my life. After all, He was the one who said, "Cut him off," so why would He call me out to Himself just to let me be killed? That would have been defeating His own purpose for my life, and Him not able to get the glory.

The plans and agenda I had for my life had gone out the window when I decided to choose a man, I couldn't see over the man I could see and had been living with for several years. So, since this is the way that I'm going, I thought, and God has become my new Man, then I need to be able to build some faith and more trust in this relationship.

Before I knew it, I was slowly but surely being separated from the man who had been in my life for fifteen years—as well as some family members and so-called friends. I started desiring to be isolated with Jesus. We would meet at the same place daily, as He started to teach me how to be in His presence. When I was unaware that I needed to be in a particular posture, the Lord would put His hand on my back and gently press, causing me to bow down until I reached the floor. At times I would be lying prostrate before Him. It was during these times that I could sense most strongly that He was doing some work in my body. I couldn't tell exactly what He was doing, but when I surrendered and was not afraid to let Him have His way with my body, I just knew from the rolling around on the floor, the uncontrollable trembles, and touches from Him that He was doing a work in me and on me.

It seemed that the more God touched me, the less I wanted to be touched by my man. Five months had gone by without any touching of each other, yet Rico and I were still under the same roof, and he was still determined to hold me back from continuing my walk with God. But my mind was made up; I was determined that I was going on with God. Something wonderful had happened on the inside of me. I couldn't explain it, nor did I understand it, but I knew that it was real and for my good.

Then came a night of testing. I didn't know that it was a test from God at the time; I thought it was the devil. The test was in my flesh because I had fallen weak. I heard the voice of my flesh which my enemy was saying loudly to me, "Just tell him, 'Yes, I'll be with you, but we must pack up, take our kid, and leave this house and check into a hotel, where I will feel more comfortable.'" As if God was not omnipresent and everywhere at the same time! I knew that God was watching me in that house, but I wasn't thinking that He would also be watching me at the hotel as well. I was so in my fleshly feelings and emotions that I had moved away from walking in the spirit realm.

Well, I followed the voice of the devil, and I bought that lie. And yes, we made up for lost time. But when the morning came. I felt so bad. I was so filled with guilt, anger, and fear that I could not get out of that hotel room fast enough. I felt as if I had gone behind my husband's back, even though I was not married to anyone, and cheated on him. Although I didn't understand it that way then, I was married I had become a part of the Bride of Christ once I surrendered and had given myself over to Him, and He is a jealous God.

After that awesome night of fellowship between us, Rico could not understand why we had to return home and go right back to the way it was before we left the house, and I couldn't help him understand. So, he hung in there for another couple of months but was still not willing to let go of his will and agenda for God's. I flat-out refused to have sex with him again. I repented for that night and got back into position with God, and I was not willing to compromise and go through that process again.

Two days before his birthday, Rico came to me and said, "Here are the keys to this house. I am not going to continue living my life like this, so I'm leaving to go with another woman because I want to be happy and celebrate my birthday the way that I want to celebrate my birthday.

I told you before, just because God called you didn't mean that He called me. He'll call me when He's ready for me."

I just stood there. I did not know how to argue with that at the time because I had not realized myself yet that we are all called by God—it is just that we don't all answer the call.

It hurt me more than I thought it would. We had been together for a very long time, even though for much of that time we had been living in turmoil, and I still loved him. Yet I knew I had to let go of that relationship. But then, in my sadness, I was quickly reminded that while he was a good provider, he was not my heavenly provider, and while he was what the average woman would call a good man, for me he was not a godly man; he had no fear of God and was a hindrance for me and my future in God. And before long, I was thanking God for taking me out of that relationship alive—in a situation where my very life was threatened, God would prove Himself again to be truly trustworthy and faithful.

Well, it was exactly two weeks later that Rico called me with a shocking threat. He said that he had hired a hit man and instructed him to come into the house and, without bothering our child, to take me out.

I was afraid, but didn't want to let the Enemy see that, so I said, "Well, you had better go get your money back, because no hit man or any other man is gonna be able to kill me. God will not let them. I'm covered by the blood of Jesus Christ."

That man couldn't even respond to that statement, and to my knowledge there was no attempt made. In that,

God taught me that He can keep me even in danger. I had been taken through yet another test, and because of it I gained and developed more faith and trust in God. I know that it was only Him and His divine protection that kept me from harm.

Now he has delivered me and brought me out of my fifteen years of drug addiction and alcohol use, and delivered me from several years of a handicapping, poisonous, and unhealthy relationship. He has guided me by His holy spirit back into the church that I grew up in from the age of six. Still, it was not the kind of church where I could openly express my past mistakes and stupid decisions I made. If you tried to talk about any kind of addiction, other than the kind that they had from prescription drugs and or so-called drinking responsibly, you were frowned upon. So, there was no person to turn to other than the Lord, and while I didn't know it at the time, that was exactly His plan.

From this point on, I continued seeking God and God alone for the answers to why I had to give up most of the people and things that He led me to give up. I even lost my mother to death, which was caused by a stroke, not God—I had learned already that God came so that we might have life, not to take life from us. The devil is the thief who comes to steal, kill, and destroy our lives. Satan is the killer. So, I asked God, what is it all about? What is it all for? He did not answer me right then, but I learned shortly afterward that it is all about Him and His purpose for the people of His Kingdom to bring heaven down to earth and have dominion in the earth and to be prosperous and be in health even as our soul prospers. We are ambassadors and soul-winners for Jesus Christ in the earth. We are the way-pointers to Jesus by our lifestyles.

During this time, I was employed at a private hospital and was working the night shift. My position called for me to be located on the main floor of the hospital, where there was only me in a particular area. There was one security guard, but he was in and out of the building until his shift was over at 2 a.m. On the same floor were the nursing service offices, and the head nurse was there every night, but most of the time she was away from the office and on the upper floors of the hospital. When I wasn't registering patients, I had a lot of time with myself. My company keeper was books on the Word of God, cassette tapes, CDs, and the front lobby television. As a matter of fact, the television was one of my greatest tools for moving me to a greater level of hunger for God. I would flip to a channel that had gospel programs on all night long, one right after the other. It was also where I first laid eyes on an evangelist that got my attention. These shows were on long after her passing away, but I became interested in getting to know more about her because she claimed to be a person who had presented her body before God as a living sacrifice. She had a true knowledge of the precious Holy Spirit. I remember one of her recordings when I heard her say, "I told God if You can take nothing and make something then, here is nothing"—I can't explain it, but something happened inside me or to me when I heard those words. I became captivated, inspired, and so overwhelmed with a desire to be like her that I started to pray right then to God about being used by Him to do some of the things she did and to be a blessing to people in the same way that she was as an evangelist through whom God's healing power flowed. You see, I found out that you don't get good to get God; you get God, and you'll get good.

I was so moved by the way that this lady had been used to doing the work of the Lord that I started calling that Broadcasting Network for information on her, asking how I could get in contact with her organization or her church. After a couple of weeks, I was able to speak by phone to someone in her church, who gave me the information I needed to start ordering products from her ministry—videotapes, CDs, DVDs, books and other products from her ministry.

This was the beginning of my desire to get to know the Third Person of the trinity, the Holy Spirit of our Lord Jesus Christ—the one that the Evangelist had put so much emphasis on and was teaching about. I learned that He was the one doing the work in my body and in my mind for change and transformation; without Him, change could be made, but not the kind of change that transforms me and lasts. You see, when you humble yourself under the mighty hand of God and surrender, the Holy Spirit will do permanent work in you if you continue to allow Him to sit on the throne of your life, and not be your own god to and for yourself. He is my helper in every sense of the word.

SEEKING GOD

I am so excited, happy, and blessed to have been chosen to be rescued and saved by the Lord and to tell you some of what He has done for me. He'll do the same for you, if you will just answer the call and let Him. He is still waiting on you.

As I continue to be led, taught, and trained by the Holy Spirit, I'm going to keep you informed on what He's preparing me to become and where He's preparing me to go and do while on this journey with Him.

In the meantime, if you have not invited Jesus Christ into your heart, now is a very good time to do so. Just repeat after me:

> Father in heaven, I believe that Jesus is the
> Son of God who died on the cross for me,
> and that You raised Him from the grave on
> the third day. Today I repent of my sins. I
> thank You for Your forgiving me.

Jesus, come into my life now. Give me Your
Holy Spirit that I may be changed from the
inside out and have salvation and eternal life
with You forever. Amen!

Praise God, you are now saved and accepted into
the Kingdom of God. You are no longer walking in the
kingdom of darkness but in the kingdom of light. You are
a new creature in Jesus Christ. Everything you have done
in your past has been forgiven by the Almighty God, and
He has cast it all in the sea of forgetfulness (Micah 7:19
KJV). He will never again bring up your past to you. All
you need to do now is to seek His face so that you may
be led by His Spirit to the very church where He wants
you to be planted or replanted to grow spiritually for His
glory and for His good pleasure. It really is all about Him
and His will, plan, and purpose for your life.

To seek Him, you might want to start by getting into
a quiet room or some place with less distraction, even if
that means sitting in your car, the bathroom, outside on
the porch, or in the park, just going for a walk alone with
earplugs, listening to praise and worship music on your
phone. Remember, God wants you and Him to be alone
just like two lovers who are becoming acquainted and
intimate with each other.

This is the time to open your mind and your heart to
Him and start telling Him truths about yourself. Really,
He already knows these truths, but He just wants to see
if you will trust Him with that information. Imagine
you just met a total stranger somewhere and there was

something that made the two of you interested enough to want to become more acquainted that phone numbers were exchanged. Both of you started talking on the phone or by internet, sharing information with each other. After a while of communicating with each other and feeling comfortable enough, you're telling that person you met some things about your present circumstances, and perhaps some of your past. And they're sharing with you as well. After communicating over a few months' time, you might even share some of your desires concerning your future with them. As trust develops between the two of you, you start seeing each other in person more and more often. As trust grows, so does the desire to share more of yourselves. Now you want to get more intimate with each other. You might even feel that you want to start sharing your bodies, becoming more intimate and making love to each other.

Well, this is what your Father in heaven wants and desires for you also with Him. He is jealous of you, just like your natural lover. He wants to woo you and hold you and love you and treat you to His special treats that you've never known. He wants to treat you like no woman or man has ever been able to treat you in your entire history of love affairs and relationships. He wants to take you places you've never been or seen before. He wants you to run to Him before going to anyone else to have your needs met. But my God shall supply all your need according to his riches in glory by Christ Jesus. (Philippians 4:19 KJV). He wants the best for you always! He doesn't want to see you settle for less than what He has created for you to have. He wants you to be happier than you imagined for yourself. He wants to show you just how faithful He is and always will be to you—not as people are, because humans can be so fickle. So, if you received Him today as your Lord and Savior Jesus Christ, then get ready for the new lover of your soul and a relationship that is going to be mind-blowing, exciting, challenging, and wondrously above and beyond all relationships ever.

I'm excited for you, and I am looking forward to growing more and more in God together with you as we are guided by His Holy Spirit in our relationship with Him. The best is yet to come!

May God's blessings be upon you, your family, and your friends. In Jesus's name, Amen!

ABOUT THE AUTHOR

My name is Charity Johnson. I am a beautiful, God-fearing African American Christian mother of two amazing adult daughters. My testimony is about surviving drug and alcohol addiction, devastating miscarriages, fifteen years of domestic violence. I now have a ministry to share my testimony to the world as an author.

Printed in the United States
by Baker & Taylor Publisher Services